ADVANCED LANGUAGE TOOL KIT

Teaching the Structure of the
English Language

by

Paula D. Rome
Jean S. Osman

Copyright ©2000
Educators Publishing Service, a division of Delta Education, LLC.
ISBN 0-8388-0548-5

GENERAL DIRECTIONS FOR USE OF CARD DECKS

There are three white card packs: prefixes, suffixes, and roots. They should be kept separated. The corners are cut on these cards to simplify this. These cards are for the teacher to use with the student during drill work.

The term "root" is used to include the segments of words which sometimes are referred to as 'stem' and/or base word.

The card labeled 'Diacritical Marks' provides information concerning the markings and format of the card decks.

Supplementary lists of less common, more advanced, prefixes, roots, and multiple spellings can be found in the *Advanced Language Tool Kit Manual*.

DIACRITICAL MARKS

Diacritical marks in dictionaries vary. The markings chosen for these cards are as follows:

ă	— at	ā	— made	oi	— oil
ĕ	— Ed	ē	— feet	ôr	— for
ĭ	— it	ī	— time	är	— car
ŏ	— ox	ō	— no	th	— thin
ŭ	— up	ū	— mule	~~th~~	— that
o͝o	— book	o͞o	— moon	zh	— mea_s_ure
ộ	— saw	ou	— out		

ẽr — her, conference (whether in accented or unaccented syllable)

ə ago, golden, (schwa—indistinct vowel sound in unaccented syllable)

-y —in final position in words such as baby, library, indicated as (ē)
   [found in the dictionary as (ĭ)]

FORMAT OF AFFIX CARDS

Spelling(s) /	Pronunciation(s)	Sound unit
[unit on	[in recommended	[meaning(s)]
card in	teaching order]	A,B, if more
bold print]	*see below	than one

Examples—number of examples usually indicates frequency of occurrence
1, 2, etc. refer to different pronunciations
[   ] indicates information concerning the unit
(   ) indicates sound of letter(s)
  _ indicates name of letter(s)
  x refers to other cards with same sound—listed in order of probability of
    occurrence

*pronunciations in parentheses are for the teachers and some advanced students.

FORMAT OF ROOT CARDS

Spelling(s) /	Pronunciation(s)	Sound unit [meaning(s)]
I, II, etc. if more than one	( ) less common ones *see below	A, B, if more than one

Examples—grouped according to root spellings and pronunciation. Pronunciation of roots may vary with addition of suffixes and some examples are given. Many of these are also covered by cards in the suffix pack.

— between two or more words separates examples showing changes of root form.

Italics indicate words using unusual variation of pronunciation or spelling of root.

*pronunciations in parentheses are for teachers and some advanced students.

-able

-**able** / ə-ble   [able]

work**able**, valu**able**, person**able**

[adjectives; any related nouns use -ability]

[usually added to words which can exist
 independently]

[used after roots ending in hard c or g
 — practical, navigable]

x -ible

-ade

-**ade** / ād

[action]
[fruit drink]

block**ade**, cavalc**ade**, lemon**ade**

-age / əj   [pertaining to]

post**age**, stopp**age**, langu**age**

-ain

-**ain** / ən

capt**ain**, mount**ain**, porcel**ain**

[not a true suffix; found often enough to be
learned as an ending unit]

x -en, -an, -on, -ine

-al

- **<u>al</u>**

-**al** / əl   [pertaining to]

coast<u>**al**</u>, person<u>**al**</u>, hospit<u>**al**</u>

x -el, -ile

-an

-**an** / ən

[pertaining to]
[indicating a person]

Mexic**an**, comedi**an**, humanitari**an**

x -en, -on, -ine, -ain

-ance

-**ance** / əns   [state or quality of being]

appear**ance**, brilli**ance**, intoler**ance**

[nouns; any related adjectives use -<u>ant</u>]

[may be confused with plural forms -<u>ants</u> and
-<u>ents</u> — peas<u>ants</u>, par<u>ents</u>]

x -ence

-ant

-ant / ənt

[one who or that which; pertaining to]

serv**ant**, remn**ant**, vigil**ant**

[adjectives ending in -<u>ant</u> use noun form -<u>ance</u>]

[plurals of noun forms — servants — may be confused with -<u>ance</u> and -<u>ence</u> words — defiance, difference]

x -ent

-ar

-**ar** / ẽr   [pertaining to]

     angul**ar**, muscul**ar**, calend**ar**

     [adjectives; comparative form uses -**er**, others
     use -**ar**]

x -er, -or, -ure

-ard

-ard / ərd   [varies]; [obscure]

cow**ard**, stand**ard**, blizz**ard**

[may be confused with the combination
-ered — flattered]

-**ary** / 1. ẽr′ -ē   [pertaining to]
      / 2. ər -ē′

         1. necess**ary**, imagin**ary**, libr**ary**

         2. bound**ary**, dispens**ary**

x2. -ery, -ory

-ate

-**ate** / 1. āt   [pertaining to]
      / 2. ət

        1. educ**ate**, evapor**ate**, sulf**ate**

        2. accur**ate**, liter**ate**, sen**ate**

        [as a verb pronounced (āt); as an adjective
         pronounced (ət); as a noun either pronunciation
         possible]

x2. -et, -ite

-dom

-dom / dəm

[state of being]

free**dom**, king**dom**, bore**dom**

-ation

-ation / ā′-shən   [action or process of]

combin**ation**, examin**ation**, ident**ation**

-ee

- **<u>ee</u>**

-**ee** / ē   [person]

trust**<u>ee</u>**, employ**<u>ee</u>**, refug**<u>ee</u>**

x -y

-ed

-**ed** / 1. əd   [action completed]
    / 2. d
    / 3. t

      1. part**ed**, unload**ed**

      [used after roots ending in <u>d</u> or <u>t</u>]

      2. seem**ed**, contain**ed**

      3. look**ed**, dispatch**ed**

      [used to denote past tense of a verb]

x 1. -id

-el

- **<u>el</u>**

-**el** / əl   [obscure]

shov<u>el</u>, tunn<u>el</u>, vow<u>el</u>

x -al, -ile

-en

-**en** / ən   [varies]

hidd**en**, gold**en**, childr**en**

[sometimes used to indicate past tense of
   verb — given]

x -an, -on, -ine, -ain

-ence

-**ence** / əns   [varies]

    sent**ence**, differ**ence**, magnific**ence**

    [nouns; any related adjectives use -**ent**]

    [may be confused with plural forms -**ents** and
    -**ants** — patients, merchants]

x -ance

-ent

- **ent**

-**ent** / ənt   [one who or that which;
                                   pertaining to]

   stud**ent**, intellig**ent**, superintend**ent**

   [adjectives ending in -<u>ent</u> use noun form -<u>ence</u>]

   [plurals of noun forms — students may be confused
   with -<u>ence</u> and -<u>ance</u> words — intelligence, reliance]

x -ant

-**er** / ẽr

[one who is; that which;
 comparative form];
[varies]

paint**er**, small**er**, remaind**er**

[when added to adjectives, makes comparative form]

x -or, -ar, -ure

-ery

- **ery**

-**ery** / ə-rē

[place where something is done; the qualities, principles or practices]

bak**ery**, pott**ery**, treach**ery**

[often combination of suffixes -**er** and -**y**]

x -ary, -ory

-**es** / əz   [plural]; [verb ending]

lunch**es**, dish**es**, tax**es**, buzz**es**, discuss**es**

[used to form plurals of nouns ending with the
 sounds (ch), (sh), (s), (z)]

[used for third person singular verbs ending with
 the sounds noted above]

-ess

-**ess** / əs   [feminine]

host**ess**, lion**ess**, count**ess**

[used to indicate the feminine form of some nouns]

x -ous, -ice, -us

-est

- **est**

-**est** / əst   [superlative form]

    bigg**est**, fast**est**, pretti**est**

    [used for superlative form of adjectives]

x -ist

-**et** / ət   [diminutive];
                                                [often obscure]

jack**et**, gadg**et**, bookl**et**

[unusual pronunciation–French–(ā) — ballet,
gourmet]

x -ate, -ite

-fold

-fold / fōld   [having parts]

three**fold**, multi**fold**, mani**fold**

-ful

-ful / fəl   [full of]

care**ful**, thought**ful**, spoon**ful**

-fy

-fy / fī   [to make]

satis**fy**, glori**fy**, beauti**fy**

-hood

- <u>hood</u>

-hood / hŏŏd   [state or condition]

man<u>**hood**</u>, child<u>**hood**</u>, likeli<u>**hood**</u>

-ible

-ible / ə-bl   [able]

　　　vis**ible**, horr**ible**, reduc**ible**

　　　[variation of -**able**]

　　　[adjectives, any related nouns use -ibility]

　　　[usually added to a root which does not exist
　　　　independently — -poss-; -terr-]

x -able

-ic

-**ic**

-**ic** / ĭk   [of or pertaining to]

cub**ic**, arithmet**ic**, fantast**ic**

-ical

-**ical** / ĭk-əl   [of or pertaining to]

    mus**ical**, econom**ical**, theoret**ical**

    [combination of suffixes -**ic** and -**al**]

    [adjectives]

-id

-**id** / ĭd (əd)

[having a quality of; existence in a particular state]

hum**id**, splend**id**, arachn**id**

[found in dictionaries as (ĭd) but often pronounced (əd)]

[may be confused with (əd) pronunciation of -**ed** — lasted]

x -ed

-ify

-ify / ə-fī [to make]

class**ify**, fort**ify**, intens**ify**

[variation of suffix **-fy**]

-ing

-ing

-ing / ĭng

[act of doing;
the thing done]

smil**ing**, runn**ing**, paint**ing**

-ish

-**ish**

-**ish** / ĭsh   [like; belong to]

boy**ish**, green**ish**, Swed**ish**

-ist

-**ist** / ĭst (əst)   [one who does or is
                          concerned with]

art**ist**, novel**ist**, neurolog**ist**

[found in the dictionary as (ĭst) but often pronounced
as (əst)]

x -est

-ition

-**ition** / ĭ-shən   [action or process of]

defin**ition**, recogn**ition**, exped**ition**

-ity / ə-tē′   [state or condition]

activity, longevity, authenticity

[variation of **-ety** following **i** — society]

-ive

-**ive**

-**ive** / ĭv   [relating to; quality of]

act**ive**, effect**ive**, representat**ive**

-ize

-ize / īz

[to make; to act in a specified way]

modern**ize**, civil**ize**, tyrann**ize**

[uncommon variation **-ise** — merchandise]

-less

-less / lĭs (ləs)   [without]

    speech**less**, effort**less**, thought**less**

    [found in the dictionary as (lĭs) but commonly
    pronounced as (ləs)]

-ling

-ling

-ling / lĭng [small; unimportant]

duck**ling**, weak**ling**, hire**ling**

-ly

-ly

-ly / lē   [characteristic of;
                                units of time]

glad**ly**, hour**ly**, gradual**ly**

-ment

-**ment**

-**ment** / mənt

[action or resulting state]

move**ment**, arrange**ment**, nourish**ment**

-most

-**most** / mōst   [most]

upper**most**, inner**most**, fore**most**

-ness

-**ness** / nĭs (nəs)   [quality or; state of]

    dark**ness**, happi**ness**, prepared**ness**

    [seen in the dictionary as (nĭs) but commonly
    pronounced as (nəs)]

-on

-on / 1. ən   [none]; [scientific term]
     / 2. ŏn

    1. butt**on**, seas**on**, compani**on**
      [usually not a true suffix]

    2. ne**on**, positr**on**
      [scientific terms]

x 1. -en, -an, -ine, -ain

-or

- **or** / ẽr

[one who or that which]
[sometimes obscure]

doct**or**, refrigerat**or**, flav**or**

x -er, -ar, -ure

-ous

- **ous**

-**ous** / əs   [full of or having]

joy**ous**, danger**ous**, stupend**ous**

[adjectives]

x -ess, -ice, -us

-s

-s / 1. s   [plural]; [verb ending]
  / 2. z

1. hats, books, disputes

2. dogs, names, excursions

[used to form plurals]

[added to verbs to form third person singular ending]

[some words use -**es**; see -**es** card for information]

-ship

-**ship** / shĭp

-ship

[full of or having]

hard**ship**, friend**ship**, statesman**ship**

-sion

-**sion** / 1. zhən   [action];
      / 2. shən   [state of being]

     1. fu**sion**, explo**sion**, indeci**sion**

     2. ten**sion**, permis**sion**, impres**sion**

     [suffix formed when -**ion** is added to root ending
     in -**s** or -**ss**]

x 2. -tion, -cian

-some

-some / səm   [like]

tire**some**, quarrel**some**, four**some**

-ster

-**ster**

-**ster** / stẽr

[one who is or is
occupied with]

young**ster**, song**ster**, gang**ster**

-th

-th

-**th** / th

[state or quality of being]

ten**th**, dep**th**, steal**th**

[uncommon variation -**eth** — fortieth]

-tion

-tion / shən   [action; state
                                                         of being]

      por**tion**, affec**tion**, contradic**tion**

      [suffix formed when -**ion** is added to root ending
      in **t**]

      [used for (shən) sound unless root ends is -**s** or
      -**ss** or the word refers to a person]

x -sion, -cian

-tude

-**tude** / to͞od   [quality or state of]

    atti**tude**, forti**tude**, longi**tude**

    [may also be found in dictionary as (tūd)]

-ture

-ture / chẽr   [state of being]

cap**ture** , furni**ture** , litera**ture**

[not a true suffix—a common ending formed when
the suffix -**ure** is added to a root ending in **t**]

-ty

-ty / tē

[quality of;
 multiples of ten]

liber**ty**, novel**ty**, six**ty**

-ward

-ward

-ward / wẽrd   [direction]

back**ward**, sea**ward**, down**ward**

-**y**

-y / ē

[characterized by;
state or quality of;
diminutive]

funn**y**, grouch**y**, inquir**y**, pupp**y**

x -ee

-ality

-**ality** / ăl′-ə-tē   [state or condition of]

person**ality**, actu**ality**, individu**ality**

[combination of suffixes -**al** and -**ity**]

-arity

-arity / är′-ə-tē [state or condition of]

pol**arity**, popul**arity**, famili**arity**

[combination of suffixes -**ar** and -**ity**]

-cial

-**cial** / shəl   [pertaining to]

ra**<u>cial</u>**, commer**<u>cial</u>**, superfi**<u>cial</u>**

[not a true suffix—a common ending formed when
the suffix -**<u>ial</u>** is added to a root ending in <u>c</u>]

x -tial

-cian

-**cian**

-**cian** / shən   [person concerned
                                        with]

     musi**cian**, politi**cian**, statisti**cian**

     [not a true suffix—a common ending formed when the
     suffix -**ian** is added to a root ending with **c**]

x   -tion, -sion

-cious

-**cious** / shəs   [full of or having]

    spa**<u>cious</u>**, cons**<u>cious</u>**, suspi**<u>cious</u>**

    [adjectives]

    [not a true suffix — a common ending formed when the
    suffix -**<u>ious</u>** is added to a root ending with a <u>c</u>]

x -tious

-cle

-**cle** / kl   [diminutive; often
                                                  obscure]

     arti**cle** , parti**cle** , chroni**cle**

     [nouns]

     [may be confused with -**ical** — musical]

-crat

-cracy

I. **-crat**
II. **-cracy**

I. **-crat** / krat   [pertains to government]
II. **-cracy** / krə-sē′

  demo**crat**, pluto**crat**, auto**crat**

  demo**cracy**, auto**cracy**, theo**cracy**

-**cy** / sē   [state of being]

infan**cy**, accura**cy**, captain**cy**

-eer

-**eer** / ēr   [person concerned
                                              with]

engin**<u>eer</u>**, volunt**<u>eer</u>**, auction**<u>eer</u>**

-esce

-**esce** / ĕs   [to be or do]

[conval**esce**, acqui**esce**

[verbs; noun form -**escence**;
adjective form -**escent**]

-escence

-escence / ĕs′-əns   [state or quality of]

adol**escence**, incand**escence**, efferv**escence**

[nouns; verb form -**esce**; adjective form -**escent**]

-escent

-**escent** / ĕs′-ənt   [state of being or doing]

lumin**escent**, evan**escent**, phosphor**escent**

[adjectives; verb form -**esce**,
noun form -**escence**]

-ese

-**ese** / ēz   [originating in]

Japan**ese**, journal**ese**, Pekin**ese**

-ette

-**ette** / ĕt   [small]

kitchen**ette**, cass**ette**, statu**ette**

[French diminutive]

-ian

-**ian** / ē-ən (yən)   [pertaining to;
                                                    indicating a person]

> guard**ian**, humanitar**ian**, civil**ian**

> [connective i plus the suffix -**an**]

> [These words are spelled the same as those formed
> when final -y is changed to i before -**an** — librarian]

x -ion

-ibility

-ibility / ə-bĭl′-ə-tē   [ableness]

vis**ibility**, poss**ibility**, leg**ibility**

x -ability

-ically

-ically / ĭk-lē   [characteristic of]

bas**ically**, log**ically**, statist**ically**

[combination of suffixes -<u>ic</u>, -<u>al</u>, and -<u>ly</u>]

-ice

-**ice**

-**ice** / ĭs (əs)   [state or quality of]

not**ice**, pract**ice**, apprent**ice**

x -ous, -ess, -us

-ile

-ile / 1. ĭl (əl)   [pertaining to; varies]
    / 2. īl

    1. fert**ile**, juven**ile**, volat**ile**

    2. sen**ile**, percent**ile**, gent**ile**

    [uncommon variation -**il** — civil]

x -el, -al

-ine

-ine / 1. ēn   [pertaining to; varies]
/ 2. in (ən)
/ 3. īn

    1. mach**ine**, rout**ine**, chlor**ine**

    2. eng**ine**, medic**ine**, mascul**ine**

    3. can**ine**, div**ine**, turpent**ine**
    [3. not always a true suffix]

x 2. -en, -an, -on, -ain

-ion

-**ion** / ē-ən (yən)   [action of; state of]

champ<u>**ion**</u>, accord<u>**ion**</u>, rebell<u>**ion**</u>

x -ian

-ior

-ior / ē-ẽr (yẽr)   [obscure]

jun**ior**, exter**ior**, behav**ior**

[may be confused with -**ier**, a combination formed
when final -y is changed to i before -**er** — lazier]

-ious

-**ious** / ē-əs (yəs)   [full of or having]

curi**ous**, labori**ous**, rebelli**ous**

[connective i plus the suffix -**ous**]

[These words are spelled the same as those formed
  when final -y is changed to i before -**ous** — envious]

[uncommon variation -**eous** — simultaneous]

-ism

-ism / ĭzm   [act of; being]

real**ism**, critic**ism**, patriot**ism**

-ite

-**ite** / 1. īt   [related to; mineral]
       / 2. ət

       1. labor**ite**, anthrac**ite**, suburban**ite**

       2. favor**ite**, oppos**ite**, requis**ite**

x 2. -et, -ate

-itis

-itis

-itis / ī′-təs   [abnormal condition]

bronch**itis**, appendic**itis**, dermat**itis**

-ium

-**ium** / ē-əm (yəm)

[chemical elements;
varies]

rad**ium**, prem**ium**, auditor**ium**

-lent

-**lent** / lənt   [full of]

pesti**lent**, corpu**lent**, somno**lent**

-logue

-logue / lôg   [speak; write]

mono**logue**, trave**logue**, cata**logue**

-mony

-mony / mō′-nē

[The condition or thing resulting from]

testi**mony**, ali**mony**, sancti**mony**

-oid

-oid / oid   [like or resembling]

spher**oid**, anthrop**oid**, paran**oid**

-ology

-ology / ŏl′-ə-jē   [the science of]

bi**ology**, ec**ology**, arche**ology**

-onym

-onym / ō-nĭm′   [name]

syn**onym**, hom**onym**, pseud**onym**

[root — usually found as a suffix]

-orous

-orous / ẽr-əs   [full of or having]

hum**orous**, vig**orous**, trait**orous**

[combination of suffixes -**or** and -**ous**]

-ory

-ory / 1. ôr'-ē   [of; a place or thing for]
/ 2. ẽr-ē'

    1. dormit**ory**, migrat**ory**, confiscat**ory**

    2. sens**ory**, compuls**ory**, access**ory**

x 2. -ery, -ary

-osis

-**osis** / ō′-sis (ə-sis′)   [condition or process of]

osm**osis**, scler**osis**, metamorph**osis**

-osity

-osity / ŏs′-ə-tē

[state or condition]

curi**osity**, anim**osity**, lumin**osity**

-ry

-ry / rē

[qualities; principles or practices of]

dentist**ry**, jewel**ry**, citizen**ry**

-sis

-sis

-sis / sĭs   [obscure]

the**sis**, synop**sis**, analy**sis**

-tial

-**tial** / shəl   [pertaining to]

par**<u>tial</u>**, poten**<u>tial</u>**, confiden**<u>tial</u>**

[not a true suffix — a common ending formed
 when the suffix -**<u>ial</u>** is added to a root ending
 in <u>t</u>]

x -cial

-tious

-**tious** / shəs   [full of or having]

    cau**tious**, infec**tious**, supersti**tious**

    [not a true suffix—a common ending formed
    when the suffix -**ious** is added to a root ending
    in **t**]

x -cious

-ule

-ule / ūl   [small]

sched**ule**, mod**ule**, minisc**ule**

-ure

-**ure** / ĕr   [state of being]

press**ure**, expos**ure**, disclos**ure**

[unusual variation (yĕr) — tenure]

x -er, -or, -ar

-us

-us / əs   [none]

bon**us**, cauc**us**, nucle**us**

[not a true suffix—an ending found on some nouns
of Latin derivation]

[often used as nouns]

x -ous, -ess, -ice

-ial

-ial / ē-əl (yəl)   [pertaining to]

filial, material, perennial

[connective i plus the suffix -al]

-ability

-**ability** / ə-bĭl′-ə-tē   [ableness]

cap**ability**, avail**ability**, practic**ability**

x -ibility

a- / 1. ə   [A. obscure]
    / 2. ā   [B. not]

         A. 1. **a**go, **a**wake, **a**musement

         [may be confused with (ŭ)]

         B. 2. **a**typical, **a**moral, **a**symmetrical

x 1. eab-

ab- / 1. ăb′-   [from, away]
   / 2. əb

    1. **ab**sent, **ab**normal, **ab**dicate

    2. **ab**rupt, **ab**ortion

    [uncommon variation ăbs- — **abs**tract]

x 2. ob-

ac-

ac- / 1. ăk′ [to, toward]
/ 2. ək (variation of ad-)

1. **ac**cent, **ac**curate, **ac**cident

2. **ac**count, **ac**cumulate, **ac**quire

[used before roots starting with <u>c</u> or <u>qu</u>]

x 2. oc-

ad-

ad- / 1. ăd′   [to, toward]
    / 2. əd

     1. **<u>ad</u>**dict, **<u>ad</u>**jective, **<u>ad</u>**olescent

     2. **<u>ad</u>**dicted, **<u>ad</u>**dition, **<u>ad</u>**journment

af-

af- / 1. ăf′   [to, toward]
    / 2. əf   (variation of ad-)

1. **af**fluence, **af**firmation, **af**fix

2. **af**ford, **af**fection, **af**firmative

[used before roots starting with **f**]

x 2. ef-

ag- / 1. ăg′   [to, toward]
       / 2. əg   (variation of ad-)

         1. **ag**gravate, **ag**gregate

         2. **ag**gressive, **ag**grieved

         [used before roots starting with g]

al-

al- / 1. ôl′   [A. all]
      / 2. ăl′   [B. to, toward]
      / 3. əl   (variation of ad-)

A. 1. **al**so, **al**ways, **al**though

B. 2. **al**loy, **al**locate

3. **al**low, **al**leviate

[#2 and #3 used before roots starting with **l**]

an-

an- / 1. ăn′   [A. to, toward]
/ 2. ən   (variation of ad-)
                          [B. not, without]

      A. 1. **an**nex, **an**notate

         2. **an**nounce, **an**nulment

[Latin prefix used before roots starting with <u>n</u>]

      B. 1. **an**archy

         2. **an**onymous

[Greek prefix used before other letters]
[uncommon variation — <u>ana</u> — <u>ana</u>chronism]
[<u>an</u>- may be confused with <u>un</u>- when not the
  accented syllable]

ante-

ante- ăn′-tĭ (ăn-tə)   [before]

      1. **ante**date, **ante**cedent

x 1. anti-

anti-

anti- / 1. ăn′-tī (an′tə)   [against]
        / 2. ăn-tĭ′

   1. **anti**body, **anti**dote

   2. **anti**pathy, **anti**cipate

   [sometimes pronounced as (ăn′tē) or (antī)
   — anti-communist]

   [uncommon variation <u>ant</u>- antacid]

x 1. ante-

ap-

ap / 1. ăp′   [to, toward]
    / 2. əp   (variation of ad-)

       1. **ap**petite, **ap**paratus, **ap**plication

       2. **ap**point, **ap**parent, **ap**propriate

       [used before roots starting with p]

x 2. opar-

ar- / 1. ăr′   [to, toward]
     / 2. ər   (variation of ad-)

    1. **ar**rogant, **ar**rogate

    2. **ar**rest, **ar**rangement

[used before roots starting with **r**]

as- / 1. ăs′   [to, toward]
    / 2. əs   (variation of ad-)

1. **as**set

2. **as**sist, **as**sortment

[used before roots starting with <u>s</u>]

at-

at- / 1. ăt′   [to, toward]
/ 2. ət   (variation of ad-)

1. **at**titude

2. **at**tend, **at**tractive

[used before roots starting with t̲]

auto-

auto- / 1. ô′-tō (ô′-tə)   [self]
     / 2. ô-tŏ′

    1. **auto**graph, **auto**matic

    2. **auto**nomy, **auto**cracy

[dictionary pronunciation may be (ô′-tə)
but students may find (ô-tō) easier to learn]

be-

be- / 1. bē (bə)   [variable and obscure]

    1. **be**yond, **be**come, **be**friend

[dictionary pronunciation may be (bə)
but students may find (bē) easier to learn]

bi-

bi- / 1. bī   [two]

1. **bi**cycle, **bi**focals, **bi**centennial

circum-

circum- / 1. sũr′-kəm   [around, about]
         / 2. sũr-kŭm′

      1. **circum**vent

      2. **circum**ference

   [uncommon variation **circ**- — circuit]

CO-

co- / 1. kō   [with, together]
                                                (variation of com-)

    1. **co**operate, **co**-author, **co**herent

    [the rule for use of a hyphen is unclear;
    a dictionary may need to be consulted]

col-

col- / 1. kŏl′   [with, together]
         / 2. kəl   (variation of com-)

      1. **col**lege

      2. **col**lect, **col**lision

   [used before roots starting with <u>l</u>]

com-

com- / 1. kŏm′   [with, together]
        / 2. kəm

   1. **com**ment, **com**bination, **com**position

   2. **com**mit, **com**bustion, **com**parison

   [used before roots starting with <u>m</u>, <u>b</u>, and <u>p</u>]

con-

con- / 1. kŏn′   [with, together]
      / 2. kən   (variation of com-)

    1. **con**tact, **con**centrate, **con**notation

    2. **con**nect, **con**fession, **con**formity

cor-

cor- / 1. kôr′   [with, together]
     / 2. kər   (variation of com-)

    1. **cor**respond, **cor**relate

    2. **cor**rect, **cor**ruption

  [used before roots starting with r]

counter-

counter- / 1. koun-tẽr   [against; opposite]

1. **counter**act, **counter**point

contra-

contra- / 1. kŏn′-trə   [against, opposite]

1. **contra**band, **contra**diction

de-

de- / 1. dē (də) [variable and obscure]
/ 2. dĕ′

    1. **de**code, **de**classify, **de**press, **de**lusion

[dictionary pronunciation may be (də)
but students may find (dē) easier to learn]

    2. **de**dicate, **de**finition, **de**stitute

x 1. di-

di-

di- / 1. dī′   [1. two]
    / 2. dĭ-(də)   [2. away]
                               (variation of dis-)

      1. **di**ode, **di**chotomy

      2. **di**vide, **di**rection, **di**versify

     2. [dictionary pronunciation may be (də)
    but often pronounced as (dĭ)]

x 2. de-

dia-

dia- / 1. dī′-ə   [through]
     / 2. dī-ă′

      1. **dia**gram, **dia**phragm

      2. **dia**gonal

dif

dif- / 1. dĭf   [away, negative]
(variation of dis-)

1. **dif**fer, **dif**ficulty

[used before roots starting with **f**]

dis-

dis- / 1. dĭs   [away, negative]

1. **dis**like, **dis**believe, **dis**satisfaction

x dys-

dys- / 1. dĭs   [difficulty with]

1. **dys**lexia, **dys**graphia, **dys**trophy

x dis-

e- / 1. ē (ə)   [out of, from]
    / 2. ĕ′   (variation of ex-)

     1. **e**dict, **e**gress, **e**vent, **e**laborate

[dictionary pronunciation may be (ə)
but students may find (ē) easier to learn]

     2. **e**dit, **e**ducation, **e**volution

x 1. aef-

ef- / 1. ĕf′   [out of, from]
       / 2. əf   (variation of ex-)

       1. **ef**fort, **ef**fluent

       2. **ef**fect, **ef**ficient

    [used before roots starting with <u>f</u>]

    [dictionary pronunciation may be (əf)
     but students may find (ĕf) easier to learn]

x 2. af-,ŏf-

em-

em- / 1. ĕm   [in, into]
                                          (variation of en-)

       1. **em**brace, **em**ploy

[used before roots starting with <u>b</u>, or <u>p</u>] .

[may be confused with <u>im</u>- when not the accented
   syllable]

en-

en- / 1. ĕn   [in, into]

    1. **en**large, **en**capsule, **en**vironment

[may be confused with <u>in</u>- when not the accented
syllable]

x in-

epi-

epi- / 1. ĕp′-ə   [upon] (variable
      / 2. ə-pĭ′   and obscure)

    1. **epi**demic, **epi**gram

    2. **epi**tome

equi-

equi- / 1. ē′-kwə   [equal]
     / 2. ē-kwĭ′

     1. **equi**distant, **equi**librium

     2. **equi**valent

ex- / 1. ĕks   [out of, from]
    / 2. ĕgz

     1. **ex**port, **ex**ception, **ex**ecute

     2. **ex**ample, **ex**ecutive, **ex**haust

    [2. used before roots starting with a vowel or
      silent <u>h</u>]

for-

for- / 1. for (fər)   [away, off]

      1. **for**get, **for**bid

x fore-

fore-

fore- / 1. for   [before]

1. **fore**cast, **fore**warn, **fore**head

x for-

geo- / 1. jē′-ō (jē′-ə)   [earth]
     / 2. jē-ŏ′

        1. **geo**physics, **geo**metric

[dictionary pronunciation may be (jē′-ə)
 but students may find (jē′-ō) easier to learn]

        2. **geo**graphy

homo-

homo- / 1. hō′-mə   [same]
        / 2. hə-mŏ′

      1. **homo**sexual

[may find (hō′-mō) easier for students to learn]

      2. **homo**genize

hyper-

hyper- / 1. hī-pẽr   [over, beyond]

1. **hyper**active, **hyper**critical

hypo-

hypo- / 1. hī′-pō (hī′-pə)   [under]
      / 2. hī-pŏ′

    1. **hypo**dermic, **hypo**thetical

[dictionary pronunciation may be (hī′-pə)
but students may find (hī′-pō) easier to learn]

    2. **hypo**thesis

il-

il- / 1. ĭl

[not; in]
(variation of in-)

    1. **il**legal, **il**luminate

[used before roots starting with l]

im-

im- / 1. ĭm   [not; in]
                                   (variation of in-)

1. **im**movable, **im**bibe, **im**patient

[used before roots starting with <u>m</u>, <u>b</u>, and <u>p</u>]

[may be confused with <u>em</u>- when not the accented
syllable]

in-

in- / 1. ĭn   [not; in]

    1. **in**come, **in**correct, **in**accurate

   [may be confused with **en**- when not the
   accented syllable]

inter-

inter- / 1. ĭn-tẽr   [between, among]

1. **inter**fere, **inter**rupt, **inter**pret

intra-

intra- / 1. ĭn′trə   [within]

    1. **intra**mural, **intra**muscular

[used before words which can exist independently]

x 1. intro-

intro-

intro- / 1. ĭn′-trə   [within]

    1. **intro**duce, **intro**spective

[usually used before roots which are not
   independent words]

x 1. intra-

ir-

ir- / 1. ĭr (ẽr)   [not; in]
                                         (variation of in-)

    1. **ir**regular, **ir**resistible

[used before roots starting with **r**]

mal-

mal- / 1. măl′   [bad, wrong]
       / 2. məl

    1. **mal**formed, **mal**practice

    2. **mal**ignant

micro-

micro- / 1. mī′-krō (mī′-krə)   [small]
          / 2. mī-krŏ′

    1. **micro**scope, **micro**-organism

[dictionary pronunciation may be (mī′krə)
 but students may find (mī′krō) easier to learn]

    2. **micro**meter

mid-

mid- / 1. mǐd [middle]

1. **mid**night, **mid**western

mis-

mis- / 1. mĭs   [wrong, negative]

1. **mis**spell, **mis**fortune, **mis**interpret

non-

non- / 1. nŏn   [not]

1. **non**sense, **non**believer, **non**residential

ob-

ob- / 1. ŏb′   [to, toward;
       / 2. əb   against; variable]

1. **ob**long, **ob**ligate

2. **ob**tain, **ob**jective

out-

out- / 1. out   [out]

1. **out**fit, **out**law, **out**fielder

op-

op- / 1. ŏp′   [to, toward]
      / 2. əp   [against; variable]
                           (variation of ob-)

      1. **op**posite, **op**portunity

      2. **op**pose, **op**ponent

    [used before roots starting with p̱]

x 2. ap-

oc- / 1. ŏk′   [to, toward;
    / 2. ək   against; variable]
                            (variation of ob-)

         1. **oc**cupy, **oc**cidental

         2. **oc**cur, **oc**casion

    [used before roots starting with **c**]

x 2. ac-

over-

over- / 1. ō′-vẽr [over; too much]

1. **over**act, **over**head, **over**estimate

per-

per- / 1. pẽr [through]

1. **per**form, **per**ceive, **per**manent

photo-

photo- / 1. fō′-tō (fō′-tə)   [light]
      / 2. fə-tŏ′

       1. **photo**graph, **photo**electric

[dictionary pronunciation may be (fō′-tə)
but students may find (fō′-tō) easier to learn]

       2. **photo**graphy

poly-

poly- / 1. pŏl′-ē (pŏl′-ĭ)   [many, much]
        / 2. pə-lĭ′

        1. **poly**gon, **poly**syllabic

[dictionary pronunciation may be (pŏl′-ĭ)
but students may find (pŏl′-ē) easier to learn]

        2. **poly**gamy

post-

post- / 1. pōst   [after]
       / 2. pŏst

        1. **post**pone, **post**graduate

        2. **post**erity

pre-

pre- / 1. prē (prə)   [before]
       / 2. prĕ′

    1. **pre**fix, **pre**disposition, **pre**clude,

      precision

  [dictionary pronunciation may be (prə)
  but students may find (prē) easier to learn]

    2. **pre**face, **pre**sident, **pre**position

x 1. pro-

pro-

pro- / 1. prō (prə)   [for; before]
     / 2. prŏ′

       1. **pro**file, **pro**noun, **pro**mote, **pro**portion

    [dictionary pronunciation may be (prə)
    but students may find (prō) easier to learn]

       2. **pro**spect, **pro**secute, **pro**paganda

x 1. pre-

re- / 1. rē (rə)   [backward; again]
    / 2. rĕ′

    1. **re**print, **re**order, **re**ceive, **re**fusal

[dictionary pronunciation may be (rə)
 but students may find (rē) easier to learn]

    2. **re**novate, **re**present, **re**quisition

se- / 1. sə   [aside]

    1. **se**lect, **se**clusion

  [uncommon variation **sē**- — secret]

sub-

sub- / 1. sŭb   [below, under]

1. **sub**way, **sub**ject, **sub**ordinate

[dictionary pronunciation may be (səb)
but students may find (sŭb) easier to learn]

suc-

suc- / 1. sŭk   [below, under]
                                               (variation of sub-)

    1. **suc**ceed, **suc**cumb

[used before roots starting with <u>c</u>]

[dictionary pronunciation may be (sək)
but students may find (sŭk) easier to learn]

suf-

suf- / 1. sŭf   [below, under]
                                      (variation of sub-)

      1. **suf**fer, **suf**ficient

[used before roots starting with **f**]

[dictionary pronunciation may be (səf)
 but students may find (sŭf) easier to learn]

sum-

sum- / 1. sŭm   [below, under]
                                (variation of sub-)

    1. **sum**mit, **sum**mation

[used before roots starting with <u>m</u>]

[dictionary pronunciation may be (səm)
 but students may find (sŭm) easier to learn]

sup-

sup- / 1. sŭp   [below, under]
                                      (variation of sub-)

     1. **sup**ply, **sup**position

[used before roots starting with p]

[dictionary pronunciation may be (səp)
 but students may find (sŭp) easier to learn]

super-

super- / 1. sōō-pẽr   [above; beyond]

1. **super**man, **super**natural, **super**lative

sur-

sur- / 1. sẽr   [above; beyond]
                              (variation of super-)

1. **sur**vival, **sur**face, **sur**render

sus-

sus- / 1. sŭs   [below, under]
                               (variation of sub-)

    1. **sus**pend, **sus**tenance

[dictionary pronunciation may be (səs)
but students may find (sŭs) easier to learn]

trans-

trans- / 1. trăns (trănz)　　　　　　[across, over]

      1. **trans**fer, **trans**continental,
        translucent

    [final <u>s</u> dropped before roots starting with <u>s</u>-
    — <u>trans</u>cribe]

tri

tri- / 1. trī   [three]

    1. **<u>tri</u>**angle, **<u>tri</u>**cycle, **<u>tri</u>**cuspid

with-

with- / 1. wĭth   [away]

1. **with**draw, **with**stand

un-

un- / 1. ŭn   [not; reversal
                                         of action]

    1. **un**cap, **un**happy, **un**conscious

[may be confused with <u>an</u>-, when <u>an</u>- is not the
accented syllable]

mono-

mono- / 1. mŏn′-ə
      2. mə-nŏ′   [one]

    1. **mono**gram, **mono**logue
       [may be easier to use as mŏno′-ō]

    2. **mono**poly, **mono**gamy

multi

multi- / 1. mŭl′-tə   [many]

1. **multi**ply, **multi**sensory

pan-

pan- / 1. păn   [all]

1. **Pan** -American, **pan**orama, **pan**demonium

para-

para- / 1. păr′-ə   [beside; beyond; against]

1. **para**llel, **para**chute, **para**dox

[uncommon variation—**pəră**′–parameter; **par**- parenthesis]

psycho-

psycho- / 1. sī-kō (sī-kə)   [mind]
         / 2. sī-kŏ′

1. **psycho**metric
   [dictionary pronounciation may be (sī-kə) but often
   pronounced as (sī-kō)]

2. **psycho**logy

semi-

semi-

semi- / 1. sĕm′-ē (sĕm′-ī)(sĕm′-ə)   [half; twice]

1. **semi**circle, **semi**colon, **semi**professional

[dictionary pronounciation may be sĕm′–ĭ but often pronounced as (sĕm-ě)]

syl-

syl- / 1. sĭl   [with; together
                                               (variation of syn-)]

1, **syl**lable, **syl**logism

[used before roots starting with **l**]

sym-

sym- / 1. sĭm

[with; together
(variation of syn-)]

1. **sym**metry, **sym**bol, **sym**phony

[used before roots starting with **m**, **b**, and **p**]

syn- / 1. sĭn   [with; together]

1. **syn**tax, **syn**copation

tele-

tele- / 1. tĕl′-ə   [distant]
        2. tə-lĕ′

        1. **tele**phone, **tele**vision

        2. **tele**graphy, **tele**pathy

of-

of- / 1. ôf′-   [to; toward; against; variable]
     2. əf-

          1. **of**fice, **of**fer
          2. **of**ficial, **of**fensive

[used before roots starting with **f**]

x2. af-, ef-

uni-

uni- / 1. u′-nə   [one]

1. **uni**form, **uni**verse, **uni**versal

vict

vinc

vict
vinc

I. **vict** / vĭkt   [conquer]
II. **vinc** / vĭns

    victory   in**vinc**ible
    victim
    e**vict**ion

con**vict**—con**vict**ion—con**vinc**e

val

vail

val
vail

I. **val** / văl (vəl) [worth, strong]
II. **vail** / vāl

value   a**vail**able
e**val**uate
validity

pre**vail**—pre**val**ence

vis
vid

vis
vid

I. **vis** / vīz, vĭz   [see]
II. **vid** / vəd, vīd

re**vis**e   e**vid**ent
in**vis**ible
di**vis**ion
visual

pro**vid**e—pro**vid**ence—pro**vis**ion

(*video*)

vent

ven

vent
ven

I. **vent** / vĕnt   [come]
II. **ven** / vēn (vən)

ad**vent**   inter**ven**e
in**vent**ion   a**ven**ue
pre**vent**
e**vent**ual

con**vent**—con**vers**e—con**vers**ation—con**vers**ion

trib

trib

trib / trĭb   [give]

tribute
dis**trib**ute
con**trib**ution

trud

trus

trud
trus

I. **trud** / trō͞od   [thrust]
II. **trus** / trō͞os

    in**trud**e   ob**trus**ive
    pro**trud**ing   in**trus**ion

ex**trud**e—ex**trus**ive—ex**trus**ion

tract

tract / trăkt   [pull]

> **tract**or
> at**tract**ive
> re**tract**ion
> con**tract**ure

tort

tort / tôrt   [twist]

con**tort**
dis**tort**ion
torture

test

test

test / tĕst   [witness]

testify
pro**test**or
at**test**ing

pro**test**ant

tend

tens

tent

tend
tens
tent

I. **tend** / těnd   [strain, stretch]
II. **tens** / těns
III. **tent** / těnt

dis**tend**   at**tent**ive
por**tend**   con**tent**ious

pre**tens**e
tension

in**tend**—in**tens**ive—in**tent**—in**tent**ion

tain

ten

tent

tin

tain
ten
tent
tin

I. **tain** / tān   [hold]
II. **ten** / těn (tən)
III. **tent** / těnt
IV. **tin** / tən (tǐn)

sus**tain**   re**tent**ive
ob**tain**ing   at**tent**ion

un**ten**able   per**tin**ent
tenacity   con**tin**ue

abs**tain**—abs**tent**ion—abs**tin**ence

sum

sumpt

I. **sum** / soŏm (zoŏm)　　　　　　[take, use]
II. **sumpt** / sŭmpt (zŭmpt)

　　as**sum**e　　　　con**sumpt**ive
　　re**sum**ing　　　　as**sumpt**ion

pre**sum**e—pre**sumpt**ive—pre**sumpt**ion—pre**sumpt**uous

struct

struct

struct / strŭkt   [build]

con**struct**
in**struct**ion
re**struct**ure
de**struct**ive

strict

string

strain

strict
string
strain

I. **strict** / strĭkt   [bind, tighten]
II. **string** / strĭnj
III. **strain** / strān

di**strict**   **string**ent
re**strict**ion
stricture   re**strain**

con**strict**—con**strict**ion—con**strain**—con**straint**

stitu

stitu / stə-to͞o   [place]

sub**stit**ute
re**stit**ution
in**stit**uted

con**stit**ute—con**stitu**tion—con**stitu**ent

stant

stanc

I. **stant** / stənt   [stand]
II. **stanc** / stəns (stăns)

       con**stant**   di**stance**
     circum**stant**ial   circum**stance**

sub**stance**—sub**stant**ial—sub**stant**ive

(*extant*; ex- stant—when the prefix ex- is added to stant,
s in stant is dropped, *stanchion*)

spir

spir / spῐr (spẽr, spēr)   [breathe]

    in**spir**e
    tran**spir**ed
    per**spir**ation
    spirit

re**spir**e—re**spir**ation—re**spir**atory

(*expire*; ex- spire—when the prefix ex- is added to spire,
s in spire is dropped)

spher

spher

spher / sfēr

[circle]

spherical
hemi**sphere**
strato**sphere**

spect

spec

spic

$$\frac{\textbf{spect}}{\frac{\textbf{spec}}{\textbf{spic}}}$$

I. **spect** / spĕkt
II. **spec** / spĕk, spĕs   [look]
III. **spic** / spĭk

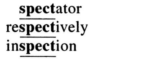

    spectator   **spec**ulate
    re**spect**ively   **spec**imen
    in**spect**ion

                con**spic**uous
                su**spic**ious

(*expect*; ex- spect—when the prefix ex- is added to spect,
s in spect is dropped)

son

son

son / sən (sŏn, sōn) (zən)   [sound]

con**son**ant   **son**ar
per**son**   re**son**ate
sonic

sent

sens

sent
sens

I. **sent** / sĕnt / (zĕnt) [feel]
II. **sens** / sĕns

    sentiment   **sens**itivity
    con**sent**   con**sens**us
    re**sent**   dis**sens**ion

sense—**sens**ual—**sent**ient

sist

sist / sĭst / (zĭst)   [stand]

   con**sist**
    in**sist**ent
    per**sist**ence
    re**sist**

(*exist*; ex- sist when the prefix ex- is added,
s in sist is dropped)

solv

solut

I. **solv** / sŏlv / (zŏlv)   [loosen]
II. **solut** / sə-lōōt / (zə-lōōt)

solve   ab**solut**e
re**solv**e   dis**solut**ion
                             re**solut**e

(*soluble*)

sect

sect

sect / sĕkt   [cut, divide]

sector
inter**sect**
re**sect**ion

scrib

script

scrib
script

I. **scrib** / skrīb   [write]
II. **script** / skrĭpt

   de**scrib**e   con**script**
    in**scrib**ing   sub**script**ion
   tran**scrib**ed   **script**ure

pre**scrib**e—pre**script**ive—pre**script**ion

(*scribble*)

scop

scop

scop / skōp, skŏp (skəp)

[look at]

scope
tele**scop**ic
broncho**scop**y

rupt

rupt

rupt / rŭpt   [break]

    dis**rupt**   inter**rupt**ion
    ab**rupt**ly   **rupt**ure
    bank**rupt**

rect

reg

I. **rect** / rĕkt   [straight, lead]
II. **reg** / rĕg (rēj, rēg, rĕj)

di**rect**   ir**reg**ular
  rectangle   **reg**ion
cor**rect**ion   **reg**al
                            regiment

(*rigor*, *rigid*)

quir

quis

quest

$$\underline{\textbf{quir}}$$
$$\underline{\textbf{quis}}$$
$$\underline{\textbf{quest}}$$

I. **quir** / kwīr   [ask]
II. **quis** / kwĭz (kwəz)
III. **quest** / kwĕst

in**quire**   in**quest**
ac**quire**   **quest**ion

ex**quis**ite
in**quis**ition

re**quire**—re**quis**ite—re**quest**

(*query*)

put

put

put / pūt   [think]

com**pute**
dis**put**able
re**put**ation

pos

posit

I. **pos** / pōz   [place]
II. **posit** / pŏz-ĭt (pə-zish)

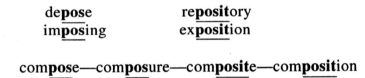

de**pose**   re**posit**ory
im**pos**ing   ex**posit**ion

com**pose**—com**pos**ure—com**posit**e—com**posit**ion

(*posture*)

port

port

port / pôrt (pərt)   [carry]

portable
ex**port**
re**port**ing
trans**port**ation

ply
plic

ply
plic

I. **ply** / plī   [bend, fill]
II. **plic** / plĭk (plək, plĭs)

    sup**ply**   com**plic**ate
     re**ply**ing   im**plic**ation
      pliable   ex**plic**it

multi**ply**—multi**plic**ation—multi**plic**ity

phon

phon / fōn, fŏn (fən)   [sound]

tele**phone**
phonics
sym**phon**y

pend

pens

pend
pens

I. **pend** / pĕnd (pənd)　　　　[I. hang]
II. **pens** / pĕns (pəns)　　　　[II. pay]

I.　　**pend**ant　　　II. dis**pens**e
　　imp**end**ing　　　　**pens**ion
　　per**pend**icular　com**pens**ation
　　pendulous
　　ex**pend**

sus**pend**—sus**pens**e—sus**pens**ion

pel
puls

pel
puls

I. **pel** / pĕl   [drive]
II. **puls** / pŭls

pro**pel**   im**puls**e
 ex**pel**ling   re**puls**ive
 dis**pel**led   ex**puls**ion

com**pel**—com**puls**ive—com**puls**ion

ped

pod

$$\frac{\textbf{ped}}{\textbf{pod}}$$

I. **ped** / pĕd, (pēd, pəd)   [foot]
II. **pod** / pŏd, (pōd, pəd)

   pedal   tri**pod**
    im**ped**e   **pod**ium
   ex**ped**ition   **pod**iatrist

pass

pass / păs (pəs)

[A. step]
[B. feel]

A. sur**pass**
    passage
    com**pass**

B. **pass**ive
    com**pass**ion

(*impasse*)

par

par / pār, păr, (pər)

[A. appear]
[B. equal]
[C. prepare]

A.
parity
dis**par**age

C.
pre**par**e
se**par**ate

B.
ap**par**ent
trans**par**ency

com**par**e—com**par**ison—com**par**able

(*par, appear, repair*)

ord
ordin

I. **ord** / ôrd   [order]
II. **ordin** / ôrd'-ən

  orderly   co**ordin**ate
                sub**ordin**ate

numer

numer / no͞o′-mẽr   [number]

    numeral
    numerous
    e**numer**ate

(*number*, *numerical*)

nom

nom / nŏm, nəm

[A. name]
[B. manage]

nominee   eco**nom**ical
de**nom**ination   auto**nom**y
ig**nom**iny

(*__nom__enclature*)

nat

nat / nāt (năt)   [born]

    in**nat**e   inter**nat**ional
      native   un**nat**ural
      nation
      nature

(**<u>nat</u>**ivity)

mut

mut

mut / mūt   [change]

    com**mut**e
        mutation
        mutual
      im**mut**able

mot

mob

mov

mot

I. **mot** / mōt   [move]
II. **mob** / mōb
III. **mov** / mōͦv

e**mot**e   **mob**ile
pro**mot**e
de**mot**ion   **mov**able

re**mot**e—re**mob**ilize—re**mov**e

mod

mod / mŏd, mōd   [manner]

       modern
     im**mod**erate
       module
       modality

mit
miss

mit
miss

I. **mit** / mĭt [send]
II. **miss** / mĭs (məs)

trans**mit** **miss**ile
sub**mit**ted com**miss**ary
com**miss**ion

per**mit**—per**miss**ive—per**miss**ion

min

min

min / mĭn (mīn, mən)
[A. small, less]
[B. project]

di**min**ish   pro**min**ent
    miniature   e**min**ently
    minor

(*promontory*)

meter

metr

meter
metr

I. **meter** / mə-tẽr (mē′-tẽr)   [measure]
II. **metr** / mĕtr (mətr)

    speedo**meter**   dia**metr**ically
    centi**meter**   geo**metr**y

mem

mem

mem / mĕm (məm)   [remember]

memory
com**mem**orate
memorial

merg
mers

merg
mers

I. **merg** / mĕrj   [sink]
II. **mers** / mĕrs

    merger   im**mers**e
    e**merge**   sub**mers**ion

im**merge**—im**mers**e—im**mers**ion

med

med / mēd, mĕd
[I. middle]
[II. heal]

I. **med**ian
inter**med**iate
mediocre

II. **med**ical

mand

mend

I. **mand** / mănd   [order, entrust]
II. **mend** / mĕnd (mənd)

com**mand**   a**mend**
  mandatory   com**mend**ation

lud

lus

lud
lus

I. **lud** / lōōd   [play, play with]
II. **lus** / lōōs

inter**lud**e   il**lus**ory
pre**lud**e   de**lus**ion

e**lud**e—e**lus**ive—e**lus**ion

loc

loc / lōk (lŏk)   [place]

local
dis**loc**ate
locomotion
locative

leg

leg

leg / lēg, ləj, (ləg, ləj, lēg, lēj) [law, bind]

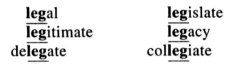

legal	**leg**islate
legitimate	**leg**acy
de**leg**ate	col**leg**iate

(league, ligament, oblige)

jur

jud

just

$$\overline{\text{jur}}$$
$$\overline{\text{jud}}$$
$$\overline{\text{just}}$$

I. **jur** / jẽr   [right, law]
II. **jud** / jŭd (jo͞od)
III. **just** / jŭst

jury   **just**ify
con**jure**   malad**just**ment

judicious

judge

lect

leg

lig

I. **lect** / lĕkt   **lect**
II. **leg** / lēj, ləj, (ləg, lĕj, lĕg, lēj)   **leg**
III. **lig** / ləj   **lig**

[I.   choose]
[II. read]

I.   se**lect**   II. **lect**ure
     col**lect**ion   **leg**ible
     ec**lect**ic
     legion
     e**lig**ible

junct

join

joint

junct
join
joint

I. **junct** / jŭnkt   [join]
II. **join** / join
III. **joint** / joint

con**junct**ive   re**join**
   junction   dis**join**ted
   juncture

ad**junct**—ad**join**

ject

ject / jĕkt [throw]

de**ject**
pro**ject**ile
inter**ject**

ob**ject**ion
con**ject**ure

gress

grad

I. **gress** / grĕs   [step]
II. **grad** / grād (grăd, grəd)

re**gress**	**grad**ient
pro**gress**ive	**grad**uate
con**gress**ional	de**grad**ation

greg

greg

greg / grəg   [together]

gregarious
con**greg**ate
se**greg**ation

(*e**greg**ious*)

graph

gram

graph
gram

I. **graph** / grăf (grəf)   [write]
II. **gram** / grăm (grəm)

mimeo**graph**   mono**gram**
  bio**graph**ical   **gram**matical
  bio**graph**y

gest

gest / jĕst   [carry, bring]

di**gest**   **gest**ure
gestation   in**gest**ion
con**gest**ive

gen / jĕn (jēn, jən)   [origin]

> **gen**der
> de**gen**erate
> **gen**eology
> **gen**etic

fort

forc

fort
forc

I. **fort** / fôrt (fərt)   [strong]
II. **forc** / fôrs

fortress   **forc**ible
ef**fort**

fus

fus / fūz (fūs)   [pour]

    re**fus**e
   con**fus**e
     in**fus**ion
    ef**fus**ive

form

form / fôrm (fərm)　　　　　[form]

re**form**
uni**form**ly
trans**form**
in**form**ation

flu

flu / flo͞o   [flow]

   <u>flu</u>id
   in**<u>flu</u>**ence
   af**<u>flu</u>**ent

(*fluctuate, influx*)

flict

flict / flĭkt   [strike]

con**flict**
in**flict**ed
af**flict**ion

<u>fin</u>

fin / fĭn, fīn (fən)   [limit, end]

> **<u>fin</u>**ish
> in**<u>fin</u>**ity
> con**<u>fin</u>**e
> **<u>fin</u>**ancial

de**<u>fin</u>**e—de**<u>fin</u>**ite—de**<u>fin</u>**ition—de**<u>fin</u>**itive

fix

fix / fĭks   [fix]

    pre**<u>fix</u>**
    suf**<u>fix</u>**es
       <u>fix</u>ation
       <u>fix</u>ture

flect

flex

flect
flex

I. **flect** / flĕkt   [bend]
II. **flex** / flĕks

   de**flect**   **flex**ibility
    in**flect**

re**flect**—re**flect**ion—re**flex**

fer

fer

fer / fĕr (fər)   [bring, carry]

re**fer**
trans**fer**red
of**fer**ing
con**fer**ence

fect

fic

fict

fect
fic
fict

I. **fect** / fĕkt   [do, make]
II. **fic** / fĭk
III. **fict** / fĭkt

in**fect**   speci**fic**
per**fect**ed   classi**fic**ation
af**fect**ion   pro**fic**ient

                fictitious
                fiction

ef**fect**—ef**fect**ual—ef**fic**ient—ef**fic**acious

(*suffice*)

fac

fact

I. **fac** / făk (făs, fəs)   [do, make]

II. **fact** / fakt

faculty   **fact**or
facile   satis**fact**ion
facility   manu**fact**ure

duct

duc

duct
duc

I. **duct** / dŭkt   [lead]
II. **duc** / do͞os

    de**duct**   re**duc**e
    pro**duct**ive   intro**duc**ing
    in**duct**ion

con**duct**—con**duct**ion—con**duc**ive

    (*e**duc**ate*)

dic
dict

dic
dict

I. **dic** / dĭk (dək) [speak]
II. **dict** / dĭkt

in**dic**ative   **dict**ate
ab**dic**ate   ad**dict**
                    contra**dict**ion

pre**dict**—pre**dict**ion—pre**dic**ament—pre**dic**ate

cur

cur / kẽr   [run]

> **<u>cur</u>**rent
> re**<u>cur</u>**
> con**<u>cur</u>**rence

cred

cred

cred / krĕd (krəd) (krēd)   [believe]

    credit
    credulous
    credence
    credentials

cord

cour

I. **cord** / kôrd   [heart]
II. **cour** / kẽr

    ac**cord**   **cour**age
   con**cord**ance

    cordial

clud

clus

clud
clus

I. **clud** / klo͞od   [shut]
II. **clus** / klo͞os

pre**clud**e   re**clus**e
in**clud**ing   con**clus**ive
se**clud**ed   in**clus**ion

ex**clud**e—ex**clus**ive—ex**clus**ion

claim

clam

claim
clam

I. **claim** / klām   [declare]
II. **clam** / kləm (klăm)

pro**claim**   pro**clam**ation
    claimant   re**clam**ation
dis**claim**er   **clam**or

ex**claim**—ex**clam**ation—ex**clam**atory

cit

cit

cit / sīt (sət)

[summon, arouse]

citation
in**cit**e
re**cit**al

re**cit**ation

cid

cis

cid
cis

I. **cid** / sīd (səd)   [cut, kill]
II. **cis** / sīs (sīz) (sĭz)

    coin**cide**   con**cise**
    homi**cide**   in**cise**
      ac**cid**ent   in**cis**ion

de**cid**e—de**cis**ive—de**cis**ion

(s**cis**sors)

cept

ceiv

ceit

cept
ceiv
ceit

I. **cept** / sĕpt   [take]
II. **ceiv** / sēv
III. **ceit** / sēt

ac**cept**   re**ceiv**e
con**cept**
re**cept**ion   con**ceit**
per**cept**ion

de**cept**ion—de**ceiv**e—de**ceit**ful

(*receipt*)

centr

centr

centr / sĕntr   [center]

central
con**centr**ic
centrifugal

ced

ceed

cess

I. **cede** / sēd   [go]
II. **ceed** / sēd
III. **cess** / sĕs

con**cede**   ac**cess**
re**ced**ing   suc**cess**ful
pro**ced**ure   con**cess**ion

pro**ceed**

re**cede**—re**cess**ive—re**cess**ion

(*pre**cede**nt*)

caus

cus

I. **caus** / kôz   [cause]
II. **cus** / kūz (kūs)

be**caus**e   ex**cus**e
causal   ac**cus**ation

act

act / ăkt   [act]

        active
      re**act**ivate
    inter**act**ion
        actual

capt
capit

$$\frac{\textbf{capt}}{\textbf{capit}}$$

I. **capt** / kăpt   [I. leader, head]
II. **capit** / kăp′-ət (kə-pĭch′)   [II. hold]

I.   **capt**ain   II. **capt**ivate
      capital   **capt**ure
      de**capit**ate   **capt**ion
      capitulate

(**cap**acity, **cap**able)

annu
enni

annu
enni

I. **annu** / ăn′-ū (ən-ōō′) [year]
II. **enni** / ĕn′-ē

annual   cent**enni**al
semi**annu**al
annuity

(*anniversary*)

arch

arch

arch / ärk (ärch)   [chief, ruler]

mon**arch**   **arch**bishop
hier**arch**y
architect

aud

aud / ôd   [hear]

audit
in**aud**ible
auditorium
audition

viv

vita

I. **viv** / vīv, vĭv   [alive]
II. **vita** / vī-tə

     sur**vive**   **vita**min
        vivid

     (*viable*)

voc

vok

voc
vok

I. **voc** / vōk,(vŏk, vək)   [voice, call]
II. **vok** / vōk

   vocal   e**vok**e
  e**voc**ative
con**voc**ation

pro**vok**e - pro**voc**ative - pro**voc**ation

(*voice*) (*vociferous*)

vert

vers

vert
vers

I. **vert** / vẽrt   [turn]
II. **vers** / vẽrs

re**vert**   di**vers**e
inad**vert**ent   in**vers**ion

con**vert** - con**vers**e - con**vers**ation - con**vers**ion